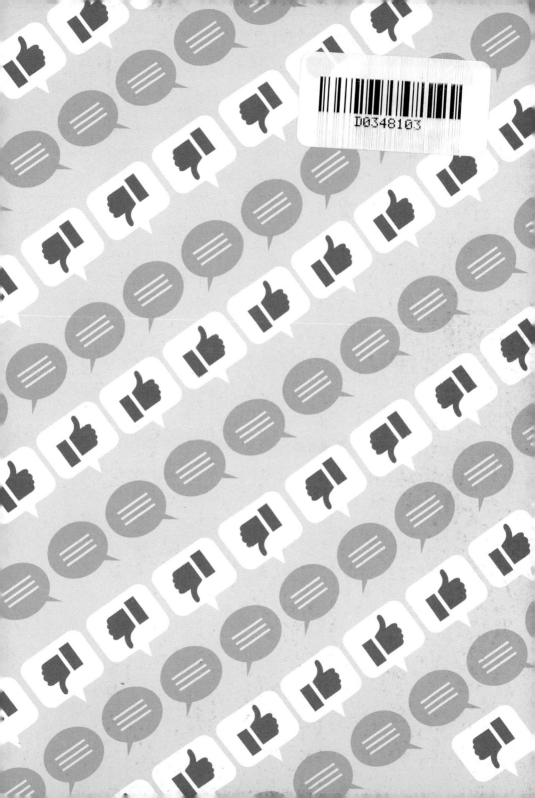

# QUESTION EVERYTHING!

Written by
**Susan Martineau**

Designed & illustrated by
**Vicky Barker**

## CONTENTS

**www.bsmall.co.uk**

Published by b small publishing ltd. www.bsmall.co.uk © b small publishing ltd. 2020 • 1 2 3 4 5 • ISBN 978-1-912909-35-3 •
Publisher: Sam Hutchinson. Art director: Vicky Barker. Editorial: Sam Hutchinson. Production: Madeleine Ehm. Printed in China by WKT Co. Ltd.

# The Information Jungle

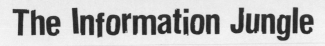

Every day we are bombarded with information!
It is everywhere, from social media to buses.

Your planet needs **YOU!**

**GOALIE GOLD!**

# DEVASTATION!
### TORNADO RIPS INTO ISLAND LEAVING
## HUNDREDS DEAD!

Sponsored

*Pooch Perfect!*
HOW to have the best-dressed pet!

 **Activity**

How do you feel when you read or hear information or news stories?

 **Scared**    **Worried**    **Happy**

 **Confused**    **Curious**    **Angry**

Some information is very helpful and interesting. Learning facts about our world is very important. It can help us to understand amazing things, make informed decisions and keep ourselves and other people safe.

'Will humans live on Mars one day?'
Exciting developments in space travel...

Learn a foreign language in just 6 WEEKS!

THE FILM OF THE YEAR!

DINOSAUR DICTIONARY
An A-Z of the ones we have discovered so far!

How can we find our way through this information jungle to discover true, balanced facts? How can we make sure that we are not learning or sharing information that is not true?

**LOOK**

**ASK QUESTIONS**

**READ**

**CHECK FACTS**

**LISTEN**

**THINK FOR YOURSELF!**

These are not superpowers. **EVERYONE** can do it!

## Word to Know

**SOCIAL MEDIA** (or social networks) are websites, apps and chat functions on games, that let you share photos and videos or messages.

# In the News!

News stories are written and shared in many different ways.
The same story often looks very different, depending on who has written it.

# MONSTER KILLER!

**Beach paradise is now a killer's playground**

**"No one is safe in the water,"** said one horrified witness after terrifying shark attack.

## Shark attack responsible for surfer injury

The Paradise Beach Surfing Club have confirmed that one of their members was attacked by a large shark yesterday. He survived, but lost part of an arm as he wrestled with the beast.

## DEPARTMENT OF OCEANOGRAPHY

**Latest news**

We can confirm that a shark was involved in yesterday's incident. Sharks rarely attack humans. It is possible that the shark mistook the surfer for a seal, its usual prey.

**?!?**

How do these different versions of the story make you feel?

**Who writes the news?**
Stories might be written by eyewitnesses or people who were actually there. Journalists investigate events and report on them. Experts may comment on what has happened.

And then there is everyone else who might want to share it!

 **Is a news story full of**

## FACTS

or

## SPECULATION?

means the writer has carefully checked the facts of what happened. They have spoken to reliable eyewitnesses and experts on the subject.

means the writer has included their own theory or guess about what happened. It might be based on the facts, but it is the writer's opinion.

**Activity**

Write up a news story. You can write about an event you have witnessed yourself. Ask your friends to read it. How does it make them feel?

## Words to Know

**RELIABLE** describes someone you can trust or believe.

**EXPERT** is a person with great knowledge or skill in something.

# Extract the Facts

How do you check the truth of what you are reading?
Where do you look for the true facts about a subject you are researching?

Check the search terms <u>underlined</u> in the text. You might think of some others, too.

## The Life and Sad Times of the Pangolin

<u>Pangolins</u> look like living pine cones. They have amazing <u>adaptions</u> to their <u>habitat</u>. There are 8 <u>species</u> of pangolin in the world. They are hunted for their scales and meat and are in danger of <u>extinction</u>.

?!?

How independent and trustworthy is a website? Does the website address at the top of the page look real?

If there are loads of strange and confusing pop-ups on your screen then be suspicious! Look out for words like 'advertorial', 'sponsored' and 'promoted'. These are like signposts that let you know that the information is possibly one-sided, or biased, in the way it is telling you the facts.

Watch out for confirmation bias!
This is where you only look for facts or explanations that back up what you know, or believe, already!

## INFORMATION BOOKS

Look up the search terms in the indexes at the back of the books.

## WEBSITES

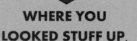

What type of website will be the most useful and reliable?

Match the website to the research project carefully. If you are writing about animals, look at websites run by zoos, natural history museums and animal conservation organizations.

Double-check your facts by looking at several different books and websites

**CORROBORATE THEM**.

Keep careful notes of the sources you have used

**WHERE YOU LOOKED STUFF UP**.

Activity

### 'Everyone should be driving electric cars to save the planet.'

Do some research to find out the facts about electric cars. You could even have a debate with a friend about this statement. One of you could argue 'for' the statement and the other 'against'. Listen carefully to each other.

## Words to Know

**CORROBORATE** means to confirm a statement or theory by finding information that helps to support or back it up.

**INDEPENDENT** means free from any influence or control.

# Disaster Dossier

When something terrible happens, like an earthquake, flood or volcanic eruption, it is important to ask questions to find out all the facts.

## The Exploding Mountain

Mount St Helens is a volcano in the USA. On 18 May 1980, a huge earthquake caused a gigantic landslide. Seconds later the north side of the volcano exploded. Rocks and super-hot gases blasted out of the volcano, along with a vast plume of ash.

57 people dead.
Thousands of animals killed.
200 homes destroyed.

## Eyewitness statement

'Rocks zinged through the woods, bouncing off trees. Then the tops of trees snapped off. It got hot right away, then scorching hot and impossible to breathe.'

Jim Scymanky, logger who survived.

## Newspaper headlines

VOLCANO EXPLODES! ST. HELENS TURNS INTO KILLER!

6 killed as Mt. St. Helens Erupts

Death toll reaches 17

Eyewitness accounts are **PRIMARY** sources. They are written by people who were actually there. It is still important to double-check the truth of what they are saying (see pages 12-13).

Newspaper stories are **SECONDARY** sources. The best news reports are based on information from reliable sources, like the people who were there and the experts who investigate what has happened.

## Expert investigations

Volcanologists are scientists who study volcanoes. These experts questioned the eyewitnesses. Their statements helped the scientists to understand what happened during the eruption. This is vital information for predicting future eruptions.

**Activity**

Imagine you are a volcanologist investigating the disaster. What questions would you ask someone who had survived the eruption?

## Word to Know

**SOURCE** is the person or place information comes from.

# Don't Panic! It Might Not Be True!

Reading the news can be confusing and sometimes scary.
But some stories are not entirely true or even completely fake!

Are giant rats running around the classrooms? The invasion might be 'giant' because there are lots of rats rather than enormous ones! This news might be partly true, but the way it is written distorts the truth.

Does this sound too good to be true? Who did the survey? Was it a popcorn company, or independent food or medical experts?

Can you believe the difference after only a week?

**?!?**

Have photos or videos been edited and changed? Can you trust the source of the images?

*Activity*

Tell someone three facts. Ask them to tell three more people. Then ask these people to tell you the facts. Are the facts still the same?

**FAKE NEWS**

can spread like a fire that is out of control. Don't share news unless you are sure it is true.

**ASK YOURSELF**

is this really true? Where has a story come from? Is it **DISINFORMATION**? Who is spreading it and can you trust them?

**FAKE Fake News!**

Sometimes people shout that something is 'fake news' because they just don't like what is being said!

# Words to Know

**DISTORT** means to twist or change something to make it seem different or even untrue.

**DISINFORMATION** is false information that is spread deliberately to confuse people or to hide the truth.

# Fake-news Spotting!

Find a story that you suspect may be fake news.
How can you tell if it is fake, true or somewhere in between?

## WHO
is writing this news?
Verify the identity of the person
sharing or writing this news.
Are they an expert in the subject?
Were they there when
it happened?

## WHY
are they writing it?
Are they trying to make
you feel or act in a
certain way?

## WHEN
did they write it?
Is it old news being made
to look like new?

## LOOK
out for the different
levels of **FAKE**.

**Lies, lies, lies!**
These can be harmful if they
make people do things that
hurt them or others.

**Hoaxes and jokes**
These can be fun, as long as
it is made **VERY** clear that it is
not true and they are not cruel
to other people.

**Biased or distorted
reporting**
This may only give you one
side of an argument or
subject.

# THINK FOR YOURSELF!

Be a critical reader and viewer. Look for and check the facts behind the words you are reading or the images you are seeing.

Cross-check them in as many places as you can (see pages 6-7 for more on this).

## Not Really Fake – Just Badly Written!

Some stories are not intentionally fake. They might be badly researched and not very well written. The facts might be incorrectly reported or incomplete.

*Activity*

Choose your expert! Match the scientific expert with the story.

**1.** Astronomer

**2.** Meteorologist

**3.** Palaeontologist

**A.** Massive asteroid whizzes past Earth!

**B.** Dinosaur bones may be discovery of the century?

**C.** Wild weather brings chaos!

Answers: 1.A.; 2.C.; 3.B.

## Words to Know

**VERIFY** means to check that something is true or correct.

**CRITICAL** describes a way of thinking and reading carefully to work out the facts.

13

# Crime-busting!

What questions would you ask if you were a detective on a case?
Crime investigators have to be really good at finding out the true facts.

## THE HATTON GARDEN HEIST

In 2015 a gang of thieves drilled a massive hole through a concrete wall to get into an underground vault in Hatton Garden, the jewellery district of London. They stole millions of pounds' worth of gold, cash, diamonds and jewellery.

?!? **WHERE DID IT HAPPEN?**

HATTON GARDEN

UNITED KINGDOM

LONDON

?!? **WHEN WAS THE CRIME COMMITTED?**

Between 3rd and 5th April 2015.

?!? **WHO DID IT?**

Chief suspects were known criminals. Some of them were in their 60s and 70s. The leader of the gang was Brian Reader, also known as 'The Master'.

# WHAT WAS THE EVIDENCE?

A very large drill left at the crime scene but no fingerprints.

CCTV in the building was disabled by the gang.

CCTV video from surrounding streets recorded the gang, including one of their cars.

The car was traced to a known criminal called Kenny Collins.

## DETECTIVE SURVEILLANCE

The police followed Collins. This led them to Reader and other suspects.

Detectives put listening devices in two of their cars and heard them arranging to move the loot. They also tracked where the thieves were using their phones. This helped the police to map their movements.

ARRESTED!

**Activity**

Find out about another crime. Keep careful notes and then draw up your own case file.

# Words to Know

**SURVEILLANCE** means carefully watching someone or a place.

**CCTV** stands for 'closed-circuit television'.

# Crunching Numbers

Numbers can be an excellent way of showing information.
They can help us to understand facts about the world or to compare them.

Infographics are a good way of explaining facts with numbers.

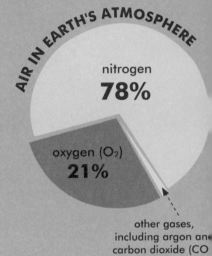

### AIR IN EARTH'S ATMOSPHERE

nitrogen
**78%**

oxygen (O₂)
**21%**

other gases,
including argon and
carbon dioxide (CO
**1%**

Bush babies
can leap up
**2.25 metres
(7.38 feet)**
in height.

This is like a human
jumping over
**2 double-
decker buses**
stacked on top of
each other.

**BIG** numbers can
be confusing and
hard to understand
or imagine.

## 2.1 BILLION PEOPLE IN THE WORLD DO NOT HAVE SAFE DRINKING WATER AT HOME.

Is there a clearer way
to explain or show such
a big number?

About **3** in **10** people in the world do not
have access to safe drinking water.

What if you read that 300 people have won a prize? You need to know more about how many people actually tried to win.

**Check the context of the number** ⬇ **the bigger picture!**

Numbers can also be used to manipulate us and make us feel or act in a certain way. Some of them may be helpful, but not all!

What do you think and feel when you read these numbers?

Numbers to get you to buy things ...

Numbers to get votes ...

Numbers to nudge you to do things that are helpful ...

**80%** of dentists recommend Tough Paste!

TOUGH PASTE

'6 billion books for schools!' say The Knowledge Party

A DRIPPING **TAP** WASTES **4 LITRES** OF WATER A DAY!

**Activity**

Find out how many languages are spoken in your class. Make your own infographic to show the information.

## Word to Know

**INFOGRAPHICS** show us information using pictures as well as words and numbers.

17

# Solve a Mystery

Sometimes we just cannot know the truth behind something, for now!
The best we can come up with is a theory that might explain a mystery.

## FACES IN THE FLOOR

In 1971 some spooky marks appeared on the floor of a house in Belmez, Spain. They looked just like faces. Over the next few years they would disappear and then come back. Were they the faces of long-dead people who had lived in the house or fakes?

## THE CURSE OF TUTANKHAMEN

The tomb of the Ancient Egyptian Pharaoh Tutankhamen was discovered in 1922 by Lord Carnarvon and Howard Carter. Carnarvon and many other people who entered the tomb went on to die in mysterious circumstances. Were they cursed by the angry spirit of the dead Pharaoh?

## DOPPELGÄNGER OR GHOSTS OF THE LIVING

Have you ever seen yourself walking along the street? The famous German author, Goethe, said he met his identical 'double' when out riding one day. Can there be an exact copy of you somewhere in the world? Is it some strange form of dream or a sign of impending doom?

Making a **CASE FILE** is helpful ...

 What have investigations found out so far?

 **LOOK** at the evidence and

**READ** any eyewitness accounts.

**THINK FOR YOURSELF!**

Be as objective as you can. That means basing your findings on facts as far as possible. With spooky or mysterious stories, it is easy to react emotionally or subjectively.

**RESEARCH** the main theories behind what may have happened.

 Activity

Create your own case file for one of these mysteries or another strange story you have heard. You might even solve the mystery!

 **Location**

 **Time**

 **Description**

 **Clues**

 **Photos or videos**

 **The victims**

 **Main theories**

# Words to Know

**OBJECTIVE** means not being influenced by personal feelings or opinions.

**SUBJECTIVE** means the opposite!

# Big Words and Scary Headlines

Some of the words used in the news can make everything sound extra scary or unbelievable. Even the way they look can give us a fright.

## TERRIFYING waves batter coast!!!!

## HORRIFIC! MAN FINDS WORM IN CAN OF BEANS!

## Power Through The Noise!

Words are powerful and they need to be used carefully. If words exaggerate, or sensationalize, what has happened, it is as if someone has turned the volume up too high and we cannot hear the facts for all the noise.

 Ask yourself why you want to click on certain stories?

## UNBELIEVABLE scenes at stadium after EPIC win!

## CAMPING NIGHTMARE AFTER HUGE BEAST SPOTTED IN FOREST!

**?!?**

How do these words make us feel?

Remember that not all news is bad news. Good news is out there, too!

## Giant tortoise believed extinct for 100 years found in Galapagos

**Activity**

Can you rewrite the headlines above to make them sound less scary or over the top? Which words need to change?

## Governments ban single use plastics

### Word to Know

**SENSATIONALIZE** means to use dramatic words or a style of writing to shock or excite people.

# Changing Facts and Old News

Facts and news can change and go out of date. Old news can be a form of fake news or misinformation. Don't spread it before you check it!

**Activity**

Use your skills to find the most up-to-date answers to these questions:

*Who holds the world record for the fastest 100-metre sprint?*

*Where is the world's tallest building?*

*How many people are there on our planet?*

*Which has been the deadliest earthquake so far?*

*How many mountain gorillas are there in the world?*

These facts will change again!

## RESEARCH

information using online encyclopedia and educational sites aimed at students.

## LOOK

at the websites of well-respected organizations like universities and museums.

## READ

information books

**NON-FICTION** books.

**CHECK** the dates of any sources you use like websites, webpages or blogposts ...

Gorilla numbers increase in the wild!
Published 9th August, 2020 by George O'rilla
Share >

Gorilla numbers decrease in the wild.
Published 3rd March, 2017 by George O'rilla
Share >

... and the publication dates of books, too.

Imprint page (usually at the front of a book)

Published by Amazing Books Ltd.
www.amazing.co.uk
© Amazing Books Ltd. 2020

**AMAZING GORILLA BOOK**

Date of first publication

**CORROBORATE** your facts! Use more than one source of information.

**UPDATE** your facts. If you find brilliant facts in an old book, search the internet for the most up-to-date versions of them.

## Word to Know

**MISINFORMATION** is wrong or false information that may or may not be spread deliberately.

# This Will Change Your Life!

Every day we see adverts for all kinds of stuff. It is hard to ignore them. Sometimes we do want, or even need, the things on offer, but not always.

Why am I seeing these ads?

Companies pay for adverts to be shown to us. Online ads pop up because of the other things we look at on apps, websites, or when we are playing games. It is a bit like leaving footprints behind us to show where we have been on the internet and what we like.

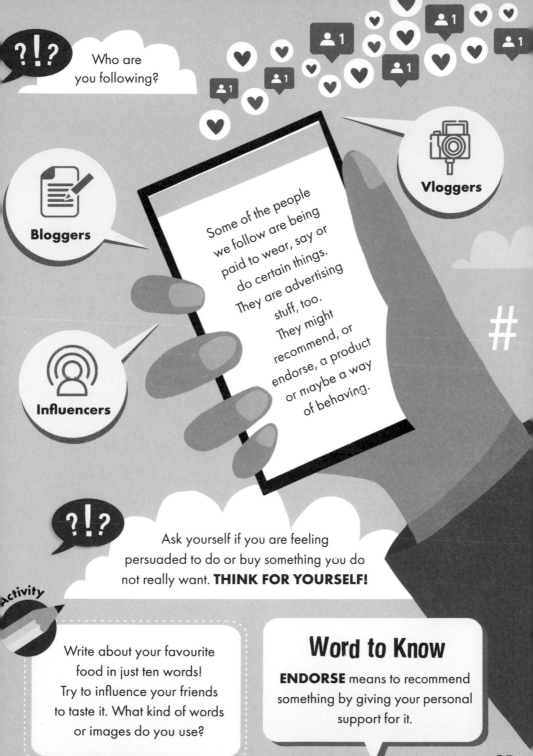

Who are you following?

Vloggers

Bloggers

Influencers

Some of the people we follow are being paid to wear, say or do certain things. They are advertising stuff, too. They might recommend, or endorse, a product or maybe a way of behaving.

Ask yourself if you are feeling persuaded to do or buy something you do not really want. **THINK FOR YOURSELF!**

Activity

Write about your favourite food in just ten words! Try to influence your friends to taste it. What kind of words or images do you use?

## Word to Know

**ENDORSE** means to recommend something by giving your personal support for it.

25

# Your Own Words

When you have a project to write or a story to tell there are so many ways you can present it.

**POSTER**

**Save the Planet**

**REDUCE REUSE RECYCLE**

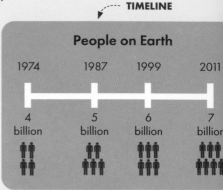

**TIMELINE**

**People on Earth**

| 1974 | 1987 | 1999 | 2011 |
|------|------|------|------|
| 4 billion | 5 billion | 6 billion | 7 billion |

**PLAIN TEXT**

**The Life of a Banana**

 Grown in hot, tropical places

 Picked and packed

 Shipped

Ripened

 Transported to shops

Bought and EATEN

**FLOW CHART**

**Activity**

**ASK** a friend or relative to tell you a story about their life.

Write accurately and check spellings. Look up any words you are not sure about in a dictionary, either a print version or online. Then **CHECK** (proofread) your work.

**LISTEN** carefully and write down the facts as they tell them to you.

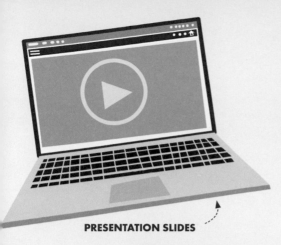

## Bring the Words to Life!

The first thing to do is research your facts to make sure they are accurate. Then think about the best way to present them. Great design can really bring your words to life and help readers to understand what you are trying to explain.

**PRESENTATION SLIDES**

**VIDEO**

## Don't Just Copy and Paste!

When you research facts write everything up in your own words. You can quote something from the internet or a book, but make sure it is clear that these are not your words. Copy it **EXACTLY** and **ACCURATELY**, and say where it is from.

**THINK** carefully about what you are writing. Stick to the facts.

**READ** the story back to your friend or relative. How do they react?

## Word to Know

**QUOTE** means to use someone else's words.

# Be Brave Online

The internet can be a great way to let people know how they can help others. It can bring people together to make positive changes.

**Walk-to-school week**

Join us!
**CHARITY FUND-RAISER**

**SAVE OUR TREES**

**BUT** what if you see mean or untrue things about yourself or your friends online?

I was only joking. Get over it!

It's not funny. How would you like it?

Telling jokes about someone, or posting photos of them that they would not want you to, can hurt their feelings. Don't post or share if you know it will upset someone.

Would you really like that being done to you?

Would you say that in real life?

If someone does not agree with you it does not mean you can be rude to them. Step back and wait until you feel calmer. Think about the consequences. Will an online fight make anyone feel happy?

## Beat the Bullies

People who tell lies about you or say nasty things can make you feel terrible. If they are usually a friend, you can try to talk to them about it. If the bullying carries on you might need to ask for some help from someone you trust, like an older brother or sister or a parent or carer.

- Remember that no one deserves to be bullied and it is **NOT** your fault if it is happening to you.

- You cannot control what a bully does online, but you can control the way you react to it. Take the power back!

(See page 31 for more about staying safe online.)

The online world is not the whole world. Be brave and have a break from it from time to time. Think for yourself!

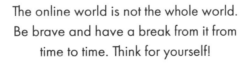

**Activity**

You and your friends could have a 1980s fancy dress party. Everyone has to leave their phones in a box by the door! No selfies allowed!

## Word to Know

**CONSEQUENCES** are good or bad things that happen because of something that is done or said.

# Words to Know

**CCTV** stands for 'closed-circuit television'. A form of video surveillance.

**consequences** are good or bad things that happen because of something that is done or said.

**context** is the wider background or the circumstances behind an event or fact that may help to explain them.

**corroborate** means to confirm a statement or theory by finding information that helps to support or back it up.

**critical** describes a way of thinking and reading carefully to find the facts.

**critical literacy** means having the skills to understand information and check it is true.

**disinformation** is false information that is spread deliberately to confuse people or to hide the truth.

**distort** means to twist or change something to make it seem different or untrue.

**endorse** means to recommend something by giving your personal support for it.

**expert** is a person with great knowledge or skill.

**hoax** is a prank or joke that deceives you. It might be funny or nasty.

**independent** means free of any influence or control.

**influence** means having the power to affect other people or things.

**infographics** show us information using pictures as well as words and numbers.

**misinformation** is wrong or false information that may or may not be spread deliberately.

**mislead** means to give someone the wrong information.

**non-fiction** is information about real people, events and things. It is the opposite of **fiction** (made-up stories).

**objective** means not being influenced by personal feelings or opinions.

**quote** means to use someone else's words.

**reliable** describes someone you can trust or believe.

**sensationalize** means using dramatic words or a style of writing to shock or excite people.

**social media** (or social networks) are websites, apps and chat functions on games, that let you share photos and videos or messages.

**source** is the person or place information comes from.

**speculation** is someone's own theory or opinion about something.

**subjective** means being influenced by personal feelings or opinions.

**surveillance** means carefully watching someone or a place.

**verify** means to check that something is true or correct.

Keep all of your personal information private: your name, address, phone number, school, age, birthday, passwords.

Don't leave gadgets lying around and logged in to social networks.

Use the highest possible privacy settings on all your social media and any online gaming accounts. Check them regularly, too.

# Stay Safe Online

Don't sign up to accounts with an age limit when you are not old enough.

If you get messages from someone you don't know, show them to a parent or carer. Anyone who would be unhappy with you sharing their messages with a parent or carer is not a good person.

People you don't know online are strangers. They might not be who they say they are. If they ask to meet you in real life, **DON'T!**

If you are worried or scared tell a grown-up you trust. Your feelings are really important. Do not be afraid to ask for help.

# The Rights of the Fake-news Fighter

The right to find the truth.

The right to have accurate facts.

The right to be protected from fake news.

The right to complain about fake news.

The right to change your mind.

The right to think for yourself.

## STICK TO THE FACTS AND DON'T SHARE UNLESS YOU'RE SURE!

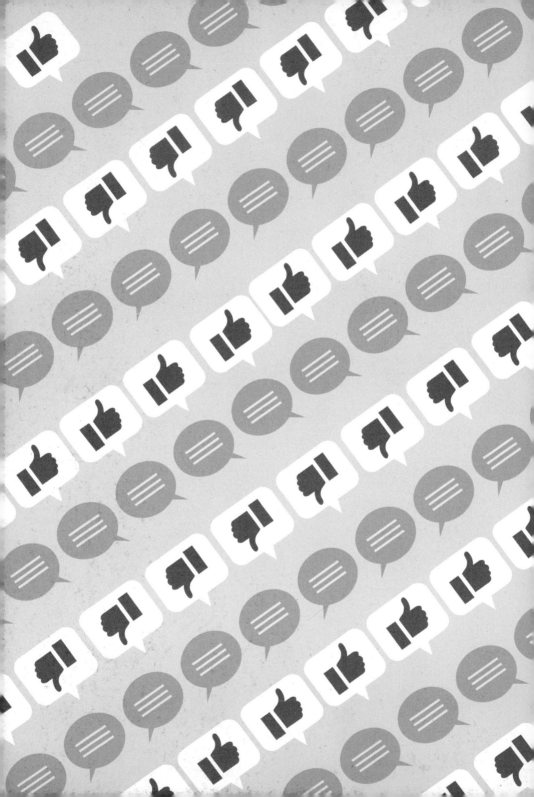